WE'LL ALWAYS HAVE PARIS

WE'LL ALWAYS HAVE PARIS

by Jill Hyem

JOSEF WEINBERGER PLAYS

LONDON

WE'LL ALWAYS HAVE PARIS
First published in 2010, reprinted 2013
by Josef Weinberger Ltd
12-14 Mortimer Street, London, W1T 3JJ
www.josef-weinberger.com
general.info@jwmail.co.uk

ISBN   978 0 85676 302 1

Printed in England by Berforts Information Press, Stevenage

For Ann Queensberry and Georges Trillat, without whom I would not have discovered the real Paris.

WE'LL ALWAYS HAVE PARIS was first presented at The Mill at Sonning Theatre (Artistic Director: Sally Hughes, General Manager: David Vass) on 24th February 2010. The cast was as follows:

NANCY	Marlene Sidaway
ANNA	Lucy Fleming
RAQUEL	Louise Jameson
CHARLOT	Michael Fenner
MADAME BOUSSIRON	Anna Nicholas

Directed by Joanna Read
Designed by Michael Holt
Lighting design by Matthew Biss

CHARACTERS

The English

Nancy, 60s
Anna, 60s
Raquel, 60s

The French

Charlot, 50s
Madame Boussiron, 50s

AUTHOR'S NOTE

The play is, above all, to be enjoyed. An essential part of the enjoyment is the use of French songs of the era during the scene changes and interval – Edith Piaf, Charles Trenet, Georges Brassens, Yves Montand, Charles Aznavour, Juliette Greco, Georges Moustaki.

In the original production Edith Piaf's song *Padam Padam* was sung by Nancy and Charlot at the beginning of Act One.

ACT ONE

Scene One

*Scene: Early spring. The top floor of a house in the
Saint-Germain area of Paris. A window looks out over the
rooftops.*

*The main room acts as living and dining room. There is a
small kitchen area. A door leads off to the main bedroom and
to a shower-room/toilet. There is a sideboard on which is a
motorcyclist's helmet.*

*Some steps lead up to an attic room above which acts as a
spare bedroom.*

*The front door opens into the room from the stairs that lead up
six flights.*

After a moment it opens and NANCY *appears. She is a large
handsome woman in her 60s. She is wearing a voluminous
dress in a colourful print and sensible sandals. She pauses for
a moment to regain her breath, then retrieves her shopping
which she has put down to open the door. She comes in
carrying two large baguettes, a huge sausage, a box from the
patisserie, two bottles of wine and a carrier bag containing
cheese and other typically French groceries.*

*She puts her purchases down on the kitchen divide, plonks the
wine down on the table which is laid for three people. She
starts to unpack the shopping. She sniffs at the cheese and
sighs with pleasure.*

*She starts to sing to herself – a French song of the 50s/60s era
– and breaks into a little dance. She is surprisingly light on
her feet.*

A male voice joins in the song. NANCY *starts as* CHARLOT *comes
out of the shower-room. He is in his late 50s, attractive in a
craggy lived-in, essentially French way. He and* NANCY *have a
relaxed, easy friendship. He is carrying a tool-bag.*

NANCY   (*as she breaks off singing*) Charlot? I forgot
                 you were here. Is the plug working?

CHARLOT   (*his English near-perfect*) As clockwork.

               (*They sing on until the refrain ends.*)

NANCY   You know, I never used to sing in England.
               Well, only hymns and such.

CHARLOT   (*sings lustily*) "And did those feet in ancient
               times walk upon England's mountains green?"

NANCY   (*amused*) Where on earth did you . . . ? No,
               don't tell me. In Eastbourne.

CHARLOT   My landlady was a big-wig in the Womens'
               Institute, – "Big-wig" is right?

NANCY   Big-wig is splendid.

               (*During the following* NANCY *is preparing and
               laying out the food for lunch.*)

               That reminds me, Charlot. What's the French
               for stop-cock? It's been driving me mad.

CHARLOT   Stop-cock?

NANCY   The contraption that turns off the
               water-supply.

CHARLOT   Ah, you mean, "le robinet d'arrêt."

NANCY   (*savours it*) Robinet d'arrêt – Wonderful. It
               sounds like one of Robin Hood's Merry Men.
               Will Scarlet, Alan a Dale and Robinet D'Arrêt –
               You know who Robin Hood was?

CHARLOT   Of course. Douglas Fairbanks Junior.

NANCY   Your landlady in Eastbourne again?

CHARLOT   No, my ex-mother-in-law. She collected his
               films.

NANCY   Yes, he was the best. All that swash-buckling.

CHARLOT   "Swash-buckling!" And you say the English
             language is less colourful than the French. (*He
             grabs a baguette.*) "Come Sheriff, show me
             what stuff you are made of."

             (CHARLOT *goes into mock swash-buckling
             routine using the baguette as a sword.*)

NANCY   Hey, careful we need that for lunch.

             (CHARLOT *puts the baguette down.* NANCY
             starts to unpack shopping.)

CHARLOT   What time is she arriving, your friend?

NANCY   Eurostar gets in at 12.17. I told her to take a
             taxi.

CHARLOT   It is now a quarter to one.

NANCY   Oh lord, my watch has stopped. She'll be here
             any minute then.

CHARLOT   How long will she stay?

NANCY   Just the weekend. It was difficult persuading
             her to come at all.

CHARLOT   I thought all English women adored Paris.

NANCY   Anna will too, once she's here. She's lost the
             habit of going away. Her husband was an
             invalid. He snuffed it recently.

CHARLOT   Snuffed it?

NANCY   Died. – A toi. Died.

             (*This is the game they play whenever one or
             other gives the cue.*)

CHARLOT   Passed away.

NANCY   Pegged out.

CHARLOT   Kicked the bucket.

NANCY   Joined the choir invisible.

CHARLOT   (*with a laugh*) No! Breathed his last.

NANCY   Rang down the curtain.

CHARLOT   "Shuffled off his mortal coil." Shakespeare, yes?

NANCY   Bravo! Went the way of all flesh.

CHARLOT   Um . . . No, I am stuck.

NANCY   There's plenty more. Turned up his toes. Hopped the twig. Pushed up the daisies.

CHARLOT   Only in England can you die in so many delicious ways.

NANCY   I don't suppose Anna's husband's end was so delicious. Anyway he finally succumbed last year.

               (CHARLOT *savours the word "succumbed".*)

NANCY   All in good time. Poor girl nursed him at home for over twenty years.

CHARLOT   Meurt. (*As* NANCY *goes to open wine bottle.*) Let me do that.

NANCY   Thanks. She was like that at school, mind. Let people walk all over her. Not that Raymond could do much of that. Not once he was bedridden. (*Seriously.*) Except psychologically. He was always a bully. First time I met him I thought "Just what Anna *doesn't* need." But of course she adored him.

CHARLOT   She was one of your pupils?

NANCY   Good lord no.

CHARLOT   You said "school."

NANCY   Not my school. No, we were at boarding school
             together in the year dot. Her parents were
             abroad so they packed her off to a . . .
             pensionnat?

CHARLOT   Good.

NANCY   And I took her under my wing.

CHARLOT   You have kept in touch all this time?

NANCY   Only Christmas cards latterly.

CHARLOT   (*drily*) With Round Robins enclosed.

NANCY   Not from poor Anna. What could she say?
             Raymond is due for an angiogram." "Raymond
             has had another colonoscopy." Mind you, it
             would've made a change from the glowing
             achievements of everyone's children and
             grandchildren. I suppose as their former
             headmistress I should welcome such a plethora
             of excellence from the offspring of my pupils,
             but I sometimes wish one of them would say,
             "My son is as thick as two planks and will be
             lucky to scrape a GCSE in Sports
             Management." Or "My daughter is a right little
             ladette whose sole ambition in life is to appear
             on "X-Factor."

CHARLOT   (*gloomily*) My ex-wife used to send Round
             Robins.

NANCY   (*scathingly*) Well she was American.

CHARLOT   Yes . . . (*Aggressively.*) Come on you cork!

NANCY   Have you heard from your daughter recently?

CHARLOT   No. I'm sure the bitch hides my letters.

               (*The front door buzzer goes.*)

NANCY   That'll be Anna now. (*Answers.*) Hello? – Yes!
               Welcome to Paris! – Come on up. (*Pushes door
               button.*) It's rather a long way I'm afraid. The
               sixth floor. And a bit dark You'll find a time
               switch on the left by the mail boxes. Oh and
               mind the first step. – Look I'd better come
               down and – (*The telephone rings.*) Drat.

CHARLOT   I will fetch her.

NANCY   Would you? (*On intercom.*) Wait there, Anna.
               Someone's coming down.

               (CHARLOT *goes.* NANCY *picks up phone. Her
               French is quite fluent, her accent obviously
               English.*)

NANCY   Bonjour, c'est Nancy Bristow qui parle. – Oh
               hello there! – Yes, she's just arrived, so come
               over as soon as you like. Lunch is ready. It's
               only cold. – No, don't bring anything. Or
               anyone come to that. It's strictly girls. – Well
               you have been known to pick one up on the
               way over. – Right you are. See you in
               a tick.

               (*She hangs up, quickly tosses the salad and
               puts finishing touches to the table.*)

CHARLOT   (*off*) One more floor. You go ahead. It's the
               door on the right.

ANNA   (*off*) Thank you.

               (*A pause, then a knock on the door which is
               ajar.*)

               (*tentatively*) Hello?

NANCY Anna! Come on in.

 (ANNA *comes in. She is in her 60s, dressed in a dowdy skirt and jacket, her salt-and-pepper hair in need of a good cut. Her manner is tentative, apologetic.*)

NANCY (*kissing her on both cheeks*) How marvellous to see you.

ANNA And you.

NANCY Are you very out of breath?

ANNA It's all right, I'm used to stairs.

NANCY Yes of course, that barn of a place. I'm surprised you didn't move to a bungalow.

ANNA Raymond wouldn't leave his family home.

 (NANCY *bites back a retort.*)

 We did have a stair lift installed. But he never really took to it.

NANCY Let's have a proper look at you.

 (*She stands back.*)

ANNA Don't say it. I know I look awful.

NANCY (*lying*) No, you look fine. Absolutely fine. A bit tired perhaps. You must be worn out, poor love, after all you've been through.

ANNA *You* look wonderful.

NANCY Wonderfully fat. First thing I did when I got here was throw out all the statins. You can't live in Paris and worry about cholesterol. Anyway the French have a much lower death rate than we do.

ANNA   Yes, why is that?

              (CHARLOT *comes in carrying suitcase and hand
              luggage.*)

NANCY   Ask Charlot – Charlot, how come you French
              eat animal fats, drink like fish, smoke that foul
              weed, and yet outlive us all?

CHARLOT   Ah, we have the secret elexir of life.

ANNA   Is it something to do with garlic?

NANCY   Or chewing?

CHARLOT   That would be telling. (*To* NANCY.) Shall I take
              the luggage upstairs?

NANCY   Would you be an angel?

              (CHARLOT *goes up to attic room.*)

NANCY   I warned you, didn't I? It's only a garret.

ANNA   What could be nicer? Thank you so much for
              twisting my arm, Nancy. I know I was feeble
              but . . . (*She peters out.*)

NANCY   The main thing is you're here.

ANNA   It's such a lovely street isn't it? The fruit
              stalls, all those little shops –

NANCY   And the patisserie right next door. You must
              try their macaroons. Sit down.

              (ANNA *does so as* CHARLOT *returns.*)

CHARLOT   (*returning*) There you are.

ANNA   Thank you so much.

CHARLOT   My pleasure. Well I'd better be going, Nancy.

NANCY   Won't you stay for a verre?

CHARLOT   Thanks but I have another job to do for
             Madame.

NANCY   (*to* ANNA) Madame Boussiron, my landlady.
             Charlot came to fix the loo. (*To* CHARLOT.) A toi.
             Loo.

CHARLOT   Lavatory.

             (*They go into the game.* ANNA *looks from one
             to the other, non-plussed.*)

NANCY   Powder Room.

CHARLOT   Ladies.

NANCY   Gentlemen.

CHARLOT   Toilet.

NANCY   Privy.

CHARLOT   Public convenience.

NANCY   Cloakroom.

CHARLOT   Bog.

NANCY   Comfort station.

CHARLOT   The place for spending pennies.

NANCY   Thunderbox.

CHARLOT   Thunderbox! Superbe. Um . . . No, I am
             finished.

NANCY   The you-know-where. The jerry. And what did
             we call it at school, Anna?

ANNA   Er – the aunt.

NANCY	Oh yes! And we all giggled hysterically whenever Mademoiselle said, "La plume de ma tante." (*To* ANNA.) You must think we're mad. It's a game we made up to improve our vocabulary. Sometimes in English, sometimes in French. Not that Charlot's English needs much improvement.
ANNA	No indeed.
NANCY	He studied in Eastbourne.
ANNA	Ah – So you're a plumber are you?
CHARLOT	Well I do odd jobs when I'm resting.
NANCY	He's really an actor.
ANNA	Oh I'm so sorry.
CHARLOT	Yes, it's a terrible profession.
ANNA	I meant . . . sorry that I thought you were – (*Hastily.*) – not that plumbing isn't a very worthwhile job.
NANCY	Half the Stock Exchange is turning to it.
CHARLOT	And plumbing can be as creative as acting.
NANCY	You wouldn't believe the satisfaction he gets from working out the intricacies of a water disposal system.
ANNA	(*politely*) It must be fascinating.
CHARLOT	She is joking. Your English sense of humour.
ANNA	Ah. (*Smiles politely.*) What kind of acting do you do?
CHARLOT	Whatever comes along. Mostly nothing.

NANCY   Don't be so modest, Charlot. He was once in a
             film with Catherine Deneuve.

ANNA   (*duly impressed*) Really?

CHARLOT   Well almost. My scene was cut.

ANNA   No!

CHARLOT   Madame Deneuve couldn't take the
             competition.

ANNA   Really.

NANCY   They say some of the best scenes end up on
             the cutting room floor.

ANNA   Perhaps they'll re-issue it with all the original
             footage like they did with "Laurence of
             Arabia."

CHARLOT   I doubt so. – Well, a pleasure to have met you,
             Madame Anna. Enjoy your weekend.

ANNA   Thank you. And for your help.

NANCY   Au revoir, Charlot.

             (*They kiss on both cheeks.*)

CHARLOT   A la prochaine. (*He picks up his helmet and
             the tool kit.*) Let me know if the plug plays up
             again. (*From door.*) Thunderbox! I like it.

             (*He puts on helmet, then goes.* NANCY
             *continues preparing lunch during the
             following.*)

NANCY   Isn't he a love?

ANNA   Where did you . . . ?

NANCY   My landlady sent him along. He does for all her
             English ladies.

ANNA   Are there a lot of you?

NANCY   Sometimes the Cafe Flore seems more like
            Selfridges. Which reminds me, guess who's
            joining us?

ANNA   Um – who?

NANCY   Rachel Hobbs.

ANNA   What, Rachel in our class with the pigtails and –

NANCY   Buck teeth, yes. Except she's no longer got
            either. Nor is she called Rachel. She's changed
            her name to Raquel.

ANNA   Raquel?

NANCY   And her image with it.

ANNA   Good grief.

NANCY   You'll never recognise her, Anna. I didn't. I
            was strolling in the Jardin du Luxembourg – my
            local park – when suddenly I was accosted by
            this amazing creature with ash-blonde hair and
            all the accoutrements. Including an Yves
            Montand lookalike.

ANNA   No!

NANCY   Yves Montand in the days when we pinned him
            up over our beds.

ANNA   But she must be –

NANCY   The same age as us, yes. (*Significantly.*) Mind,
            you, she takes regular trips to South Africa.

ANNA   What?

NANCY   Haven't you noticed how many women go off
            "on safari" these days?

ANNA   No.

NANCY   They disappear for a month, come back looking ten years younger. And without having glimpsed a lizard, let alone a leopard.

ANNA   You mean . . . ?

NANCY   Yes. They stay in some expensive clinic and lie low till the scars have healed.

ANNA   And Rachel's been . . . ?

NANCY   Nipped, tucked, enhanced.

ANNA   (*with disbelief*) That funny little creature. Imagine! Mind you she was a bit of a show-off at school.

NANCY   Wasn't she just? Used to flash her knickers at the drop of a hat. Still does come to that. And they're not navy blue serge now. Anyway it turned out she's was living here too, just round the corner. I won't pretend we're soul mates. She's the kind of female I thoroughly disapprove of. But somehow, when one's in Paris . . . (*She sighs contentedly.*)

ANNA   And she's coming to lunch?

NANCY   Yes. Incidentally you do eat foie gras?

ANNA   Well – er . . .

NANCY   Don't tell me you're an animal rights fanatic.

ANNA   It's not that. Only . . . Raymond was on a very strict diet. So for the last few years I've tended –

NANCY   To eat what he ate.

ANNA   It seemed only fair.

NANCY   And what did he eat?

ANNA   Boiled fish mostly.

NANCY   You're a saint, Anna.

ANNA   No, I'm not. It was just simpler. And now and
          then I did break out and have a surreptitious –

NANCY   Steak Diane?

ANNA   Lamb chop.

NANCY   You've come to the right place, my girl. They
          do divine cotelettes at the bistrot two doors
          down.

ANNA   I can't believe I'm really here. It's all so . . .
          French.

NANCY   (*with a contented sigh*) Yes.

ANNA   Funny, I always thought of you as essentially
          English.

NANCY   So did I. I suppose there was always a
          Parisienne manquée struggling to get out.
          Since I came here I seem to have – what's that
          loathsome expression – "Found myself."
          Conjures up a vision of – me, walking along the
          street and suddenly spotting a miniature
          version of myself lying in the gutter like a lost
          glove.

ANNA   Only waving enthusiastically.

NANCY   And doing the Can-Can!

ANNA   Is that how it happened? A Road to Damascus
          flash?

NANCY   More of a Road *from* Haselmere. I could've
          stayed on in my cottage after I retired, sat on
          various committees, been a pillar of society.

ANNA   I'm sure you were much in demand.

NANCY   Yes, but I was so tired of meetings and
                paperwork and targets. I'd turned the school
                around, and I realised it was time to turn myself
                around. After all I could go on for another
                thirty years. "Is that how I want to end my
                days?" I asked myself. "Rushing home from
                committees to watch *Countdown*."

ANNA   What made you choose Paris?

NANCY   Lots of things. One can always pop back and
                forth on the good old Eurostar. And then I
                suppose – shades of one's youth. Remember
                how exotic it all seemed back then? Francoise
                Sagan, Simone Signoret, Alain Delon – and the
                songs – Piaf, Charles Trenet, Georges Brassens –

ANNA   Charles Aznavour!

NANCY   It was all a far away dream then. No Channel
                Tunnel. Then later I'd see my pupils go off
                there to study French or History of Art, and
                when they came back they'd acquired a certain
                . . . je ne sais quoi. A new dimension. I used to
                feel a little envious. Oh, I'd been here for the
                odd weekend break, to see an exhibition or
                something. But actually to live here. So I
                thought, why not? It's now or never.

ANNA   And you took the plunge?

NANCY   Well, dipped a tentative toe in first. Came over
                for a week or two at a time. I used to find – the
                minute the train was through the tunnel and
                into France – I felt a sense of elation. I don't
                know if it was the smell of coffee or the fields
                or hearing their beautiful language. Or simply
                the sensation of breaking out. All my life I've
                been institutionalised. My whole life up to now
                – has been ruled by a timetable. Since I came
                here I've felt free for the first time ever.

ANNA	Have you sold your house?
NANCY	Let it. Just in case. I rent this from Madame Boussiron. She specialises in "les dames anglaises." Raquel has one of her flats too.
ANNA	What's she like?
NANCY	Madame Boussiron? Typical Parisienne. (*Beat*.) A bitch.
ANNA	But surely . . .
NANCY	You can love Paris without loving all its inhabitants. She takes a sadistic pleasure in putting one down. If you speak English she takes offence. If you speak French she corrects you.

(ANNA *smiles*.)

NANCY	What's your French like these days?
ANNA	Pretty well non-existent. Just a few remnants of the stuff we learnt at school.
NANCY	You'll soon pick it up.
ANNA	In three days?
NANCY	Have you any health problems?
ANNA	No.
NANCY	Pity.
ANNA	Why?
NANCY	Best place to practice the lingo is a pharmacy. Nothing the French like more than discussing their ailments. My bladder was my passport to acceptance in Paris.

ANNA   (*concerned*) You've bladder trouble?

NANCY   With the plumbing here? Heaven forfend. But
               they don't know that. Hey, you haven't seen
               your room yet. Come on up before Raquel
               arrives. (*As* ANNA *follows her up the stairs.*)
               There's a marvellous view of the rooftops. If
               you lean out far enough you can see Notre
               Dame. If you don't break your neck first.

               (*They go into the attic room. A pause. Then the
               outside door opens and* RAQUEL *enters. She is
               as* NANCY *described. Ash blonde with a
               too-short skirt and décolleté top. She is
               carrying her stilettos. She leans against the
               doorframe pausing to take strangulated
               breaths.*)

RAQUEL   (*comes in*) Nancy! (*Seeing no one is there.*)
               Nancy?

NANCY   Raquel? Up here. We'll be down in a tick. Make
               yourself at home.

RAQUEL   Will do.

               (RAQUEL *puts on her stilettos, displaying a lot
               of leg, then she goes to look at the table, dips
               her finger in the foie gras and licks it, pours
               herself a glass of wine, sits down, takes out
               her mobile and dials.*)

RAQUEL   (*getting message*) Jean-Claude? 'ello, chérie,
               c'est moi . . . (*With a note of desperation.*) Ou
               est-tu? Je t'ai appelé plus de mille fois. Tu n'as
               pas eu mes autres messages? Appelez-moi
               dès que tu peux.

NANCY   (*on stairs, followed by* ANNA) Sorry to keep
               you, Raquel.

RAQUEL   (*on mobile with a quick change of voice*)
               Aurevoir, chérie. A bientôt. (*Blows him kisses,
               then switches off.*) Jean-Claude. He

can't leave me alone. – Well come on, where is
she? I'm dying to see her.

NANCY   Anna, come and meet Raquel.

(ANNA *appears on the stairs.*)

ANNA   (*tentatively*) Hello.

RAQUEL   Good God, you look dreadful.

(*Blackout. Pause. Laughter. Lights up. Half an
hour later. They are all seated at the table
having lunch.*)

RAQUEL   So tell me what you've been up to all these
years, Annie?

ANNA   Nothing really.

RAQUEL   Come on, last time we met you were off to Mrs
Somebody's Secretarial Academy, You must've
done something since then.

ANNA   I got married.

RAQUEL   I hope you had better luck than I did.

(NANCY *gives her a meaningful look.*)

RAQUEL   Oh lord yes, Nancy did tell me. You've been
doing your Florence Nightingale bit for yoinks.
How ghastly for you.

ANNA   It was worse for him.

RAQUEL   You must be an absolute saint.

ANNA   (*edgy*) I wish everyone would stop saying that,
I did what anyone would have done.

RAQUEL   Not me. I'd have put something in his cocoa.

NANCY   Raquel!

RAQUEL	Sorry but I'm squeamish about illness of any sort. Can't even stand it when a man blows his nose. The way they examine their handkerchiefs afterwards.
NANCY	Not in the middle of lunch.
ANNA	What about you, Rachel?
RAQUEL	Raquel.
ANNA	Sorry. I'm sure your life's been far more interesting.
RAQUEL	Where to start? I seem to've spent most of it getting hitched or unhitched. Thought of writing a book called "Hitchhiker's Guide to the Phallicsy."
NANCY	How many husbands was it?
RAQUEL	Five.
NANCY	So far.
RAQUEL	Ah, no! I've learnt the error of my ways.
ANNA	Did you say *five*?
RAQUEL	Approximately. The first was Reggie. He was the nicest by far. But nice is so dull when you're twenty. Then there was Alec. He was bi-sexual. I never knew where I was with him. I knew where I was with Philip. Chained to the bedpost most of the time. He was into S and M. He had a coronary on the job.
ANNA	How dreadful.
RAQUEL	Yes, you try dialling 999, gagged and in handcuffs. How many's that?
ANNA	Three.

RAQUEL   Let's see now. Divorced, annulled, died – um –
            divorced – no!

NANCY   Beheaded?

RAQUEL   I wish. Bastard turned out to be a bigamist.

NANCY   If you must marry a long-distance lorry driver.

RAQUEL   He wasn't a driver. He owned the whole fleet.

ANNA   What about Number Five?

RAQUEL   Impotent. And he was allergic to Viagra. In the
            end I said, "Why not stick to wanking?" Could
            you pass the foie gras?

            (NANCY *does so, unamused.*)

NANCY   Personally I've never known why people are so
            obsessed with sex.

RAQUEL   Don't suppose you had much chance to find
            out. Headmistress of a girls' boarding school.

NANCY   (*significantly*) I did have holidays.

            (*They both look at her.*)

RAQUEL   Don't tell me you were the Shirley Valentine of
            Haselmere.

NANCY   I had the odd skirmish.

ANNA   You make it sound like a battle!

NANCY   It is in a way isn't it? Sex. All that thrusting
            and parrying. And, like war, completely
            unnecessary. Except for the procreation of
            children. And I had more than enough of them
            through my hands.

RAQUEL   It may not be necessary, but it's damn good
           fun. Especially when you reach the age of no
           return. As far as I'm concerned the menopause
           was womens' liberation. Have you any kids,
           Anna?

ANNA   (*a sore point*) No, I'd – we'd like to have had
           there, but – we put it off to begin with because
           of Raymond's career. He'd just been made a
           partner. And then – later – we tried, but – and
           when he became ill it just wasn't practical.

NANCY   Of course not.

ANNA   What about you, Raquel? Did you have
           children?

RAQUEL   Four. And umpteen grandchildren, scattered all
           over the world so I hardly ever see them.

NANCY   (*pointedly*) Except the one in South Africa.

RAQUEL   (*to* ANNA) Oh yes, we go on safari sometimes.
           Have you ever been? The wild open spaces,
           the animals. Nothing like it. I come back a new
           woman. (NANCY *and* ANNA *exchange looks.*)
           But give me Paris any day. Here you can play
           the field without compunction. Women of our
           age aren't invisible like they are in England.
           Frenchmen appreciate the older woman. Just as
           they like their cheese ripe.

           (*Her mobile rings. A horrid little jingle.*)

           (*to* NANCY *and* ANNA) Excuse me. (*On phone.*)
           'Ello? – Ah, c'est toi, chéri . . . Je t'ai dit. – Je
           suis avec mes amies anglaises. (*To the others.*)
           Checking up on me as usual! (*On phone.*)
           Amies d'école . . . Non, c'est la vérité". Je le
           promets . . . Ce soir? Oui. Chez moi. (*She
           laughs sexily.*) Non, ce n'est pas leur true . . .
           A bientôt. (*As she switches off mobile, to*
           ANNA.) Jean-Claude, my toyboy. He wanted me
           to ask you round for a "partouse."

ANNA   What's that?

NANCY   (*hastily*) An aperitif.

RAQUEL   A gang-bang. Honestly, Nancy, we're not at
           school now. Anyway, I declined on your
           behalf. (*Picking up wine bottle.*) Shall I help
           myself! (*She does so before* NANCY *can reply.*)

NANCY   Feel free.

RAQUEL   Another glass for you, Anna?

ANNA   I'd better not.

RAQUEL   Go on. You're not driving.

ANNA   I'm not too used to drinking. Raymond wasn't
           allowed alcohol so –

NANCY   A soupçon won't hurt you.

ANNA   I mustn't get into bad habits.

RAQUEL   Why not? You're in Paris now.

NANCY   And you can't go far off the rails in one
           weekend.

RAQUEL   Can't you just!

ANNA   Only a drop. (*As* RAQUEL *pours.*) Stop!

NANCY   I wish you could stay longer, Anna.

RAQUEL   Yes, Paris is just what you need.

NANCY   There's so much to see and do.

ANNA   It's very sweet of you but – I can't –

NANCY   Whyever not?

ANNA	Well for a start – I've got my return ticket for Eurostar.
RAQUEL	Bugger Eurostar.
NANCY	You don't have anyone else to think of now, do you?
ANNA	No, but –
NANCY	Come on, it'd give you a chance to unwind.
RAQUEL	And have a decent haircut.
NANCY	I 'll take you to some galleries.
RAQUEL	You can splurge out a bit.
NANCY	I can show you the *real* Paris.
RAQUEL	I know some marvellous dress shops. I bet you haven't bought yourself anything new for years.
ANNA	Well no but –
RAQUEL	Go on, stay for a couple of weeks.
NANCY	I'd love to have you, Annie. It's time someone looked after you for a change.
RAQUEL	Yes, you could do with some TLC.
NANCY	Come on. What do you say?

(ANNA *bursts into tears.*)

Blackout – French song.

Scene Two

The same. A few days later.

CHARLOT *comes out of the shower-room. He puts on coffee,
takes tool out of bag and goes back into the shower-room.*

After a moment ANNA *comes in from the outside door. She has
had her hair cut in a becoming style and looks younger and
more relaxed. She is wearing a simple skirt and a blouse and
is carrying a "Galerie Lafayette" bag. She puts it down and
takes out an attractive scarf. She stands in front of the mirror
and drapes it round her shoulders. She tries several times to
achieve the "French look" but fails. She sighs frustratedly.*

The cafetière bubbles and switches itself off. ANNA *reacts, as
She realises that she is not alone.*

ANNA	(*calls*) Nancy?
CHARLOT	(*coming out of shower-room*) Elle est partie à son cours de yoga. Puis-je vous aid – (*He breaks off as he recognises* ANNA.) Madame Anna!
ANNA	Oh, bonjour, Chariot. (*Awkwardly.*) Je fais – non – er . . . je faisais mes achats chez "Lafayette".
CHARLOT	(*fast*) Je ne vous avais pas reconnu. Vous vous êtes fait couper les cheveux, n'est-ce pas? Cela vous va à merveille.
ANNA	Sorry, I'm afraid my French isn't up to that.
CHARLOT	I didn't recognise you. You have a new hairstyle.
ANNA	(*self-conscious*) Oh yes.
CHARLOT	You look ten years younger.
ANNA	(*anxiously*) Is it too juvenile? I did try to tell her, but I didn't know the French for "just a trim" and she –
CHARLOT	(*laughs*) You English can never take the compliment. I mean you look fabulous.

ANNA	Thank you. (*Beat.*) Is it the lavatory plug again?
CHARLOT	No, the shower.
ANNA	Oh yes, Nancy said she was going to report it to the landlady. Madame – er . . .
CHARLOT	Boussiron. I was at her house when Nancy phoned. I'm doing some decorating there. Coffee? I just made some.
ANNA	Thanks.
CHARLOT	(*as he sees to coffee*) I thought you were going back on Monday.
ANNA	Nancy and Raquel persuaded me to stay on a bit longer.
CHARLOT	Splendid.
ANNA	Do you know Raquel?
CHARLOT	Everyone knows Raquel. Milk?
ANNA	No thank you.
	(*A pause as they drink their coffee.*)
CHARLOT	(*delicately*) I believe your husband . . . has recently snuffed it.
	(ANNA *stifles a laugh in spite of herself, putting her hand over her mouth, a habit she has when she laughs.*)
CHARLOT	"Snuffed it" is not right? It means died, no?
ANNA	Yes. At least –
CHARLOT	The wrong sort of died?

ANNA   Well . . .

CHARLOT   "Pushed up the daisies" would be better?

ANNA   (*laughs again*) No!

CHARLOT   "Turned up his toes?"

ANNA   (*through laughter*) I'm sorry, I shouldn't
            laugh.

CHARLOT   Yes you should. On Friday you were looking so
            sad.

ANNA   (*beat*) I think I will have a little milk.

            (*He passes carton.*)

CHARLOT   So what should I have said? Your husband he
            has died?

ANNA   That's probably safest. All the other ways
            have different connotations.

CHARLOT   The English language is so beautifully
            complicated. Like the English women.

ANNA   You think so?

CHARLOT   I know so, after a year in Eastbourne. On the
            surface they are polite, reserved, but
            underneath they are . . . "smouldering" with
            emotion.

ANNA   I've never been to Eastbourne. I hear it's very
            pleasant.

CHARLOT   "England's green and pleasant land." (*Beat.*) I
            am sorry about your husband.

ANNA   Thank you. He'd been ill for a very long time,
            so in some respects . . .

CHARLOT   A blessed release?

ANNA   I suppose so.

CHARLOT   (*pause*) It must have left a big hole in your life.

ANNA   I'd been with him since I was twenty.

CHARLOT   (*empathising*) To lose someone you love is the worst thing . . .

ANNA   You've lost someone too?

CHARLOT   My little girl.

ANNA   No! Oh Charlot, how awful. – How did she die?

CHARLOT   Oh she's not dead. Almost as bad. She lives in Florida.

ANNA   You're divorced?

CHARLOT   Yes – for five years now. (*With feeling*.) I blame Chirac.

ANNA   For the breakdown of your marriage?

CHARLOT   Maybe not entirely. Cheryl had realised already that I was not France's answer to Johnny Depp. But Chirac was the straw that broke the . . . camel's back?

ANNA   That's right.

CHARLOT   Cheryl is American, you see. When Chirac stood up against the Iraq invasion – the one good thing he ever did! – there was civil war in our home. The woman went crazy. She even tried to boycott French wine. In Paris! And the worst, she makes Lottie wear a t-shirt saying "I'm backing Bush". And all this while I am giving my one-man show on, "The Pity of War." – In the end we agreed to a temporary separation. Temporary, ha! She went back to the States. Next thing I know, she is wanting a

divorce so she can marry this "big-wig" in real
estate. It is bad enough that Lottie has a
stepfather, but one with a name like Chuck . . . !

ANNA   (*smiles sympathetically*) You have joint
            custody, do you?

CHARLOT   Not any more. My lifestyle was considered
            "unsuitable" for a child. They say Cheryl and
            Chuck can give her a more "stable
            environment." She has grandparents over there
            too, with a condominium in Palm Beach.

ANNA   What about visiting rights?

CHARLOT   It is not so cheap to go out there. And if I did,
            Lottie must have a chaperone.

ANNA   Whatever for?

CHARLOT   Cheryl took out some sort of "safety order"
            after she stayed with me in Paris two years ago.

ANNA   Why?

CHARLOT   She fell off the back of my motorbike.

ANNA   Oh Charlot. Was she badly hurt?

CHARLOT   No, it was parked at the time. I was though. I
            went to catch her and slipped a disc. – And
            then there was the question of "passive
            smoking." They accused me of aggravating her
            asthma.

ANNA   Do you smoke heavily?

CHARLOT   I don't smoke at all. Can't afford to. But they
            said I "subjected her to polluted atmospheres."

ANNA   And did you?

CHARLOT   Well, I was performing in a bar at the time. That
            was before they banned smoking. I couldn't

leave her on her own, could I? Maybe I am not the ideal father, but I love her. She is my daughter, not Chuck's.

ANNA   When she is older she'll be able to choose for herself.

CHARLOT   By then she'll be a plastic Barbie doll who thinks Culture is rushing round the world buying postcards.

                (ANNA *laughs, her hand goes to her mouth.*)

CHARLOT   Why do you do that?

ANNA   What?

CHARLOT   (*moving to kneel beside her chair*) Put your hand over your mouth whenever you smile.

ANNA   Do I?

CHARLOT   As if to hide your lips.

ANNA   I didn't realise . . . Maybe it's because my – someone once told me – a long time ago – that my mouth was crooked.

CHARLOT   But your mouth is par faite.

                (*A pause, then* NANCY *comes in wearing her yoga outfit. She takes in their proximity, then comes in leaving the door open.*)

NANCY   (*sniffing it*) Ah, coffee, wonderful!

ANNA   Hello, Nancy.

CHARLOT   How was your yoga?

NANCY   Bliss. I haven't yet mastered the lotus position but my "tortoise" is coming on apace. (*As she turns to pour coffee.*) Which has to be an oxymoron.

(ANNA *laughs, her hand goes automatically to
her mouth, then she remembers, looks at*
CHARLOT *and removes it. He nods with
approval.*)

ANNA   I'd better take my things upstairs.

            (*She picks up the shopping bag.*)

NANCY   See you in a tick. (*As* ANNA *goes up the stairs.*)
            Don't forget we're going to the Rodin this
            afternoon. (*Sotto, to* CHARLOT.) Charlot, I hope
            you weren't trying it on with Anna.

CHARLOT   Trying what on?

NANCY   Your hammy seduction routine.

CHARLOT   I was only talking to her. And what do you
            mean "hammy?"

NANCY   You do tend to go over the top. And abseil
            down the other side for two pins.

CHARLOT   Who, me?

NANCY   (*amused as she recalls the occasion*)
            Remember when you tried to chat me up?

CHARLOT   You never let me forget it.

NANCY   (*mimicking him*) "You are like a luscious
            full-blown rose, ripe for the picking."

CHARLOT   (*indignant*) And you laughed at me.

NANCY   Which is why we are still friends.

CHARLOT   That line went down well in Eastbourne.

            (*They both laugh.*)

NANCY   The shower all right?

CHARLOT	Yes. It was only a loose connection. I'll check it once more.
	(*He goes into the shower-room.* ANNA *comes down the stairs carrying a parcel.*)
ANNA	You were right about the pharmacy. I spent twenty five minutes discussing my blisters. – A toi! In French.
NANCY	Blisters? No, haven't a clue.
ANNA	Cloque. Ampoule. Phyltène. Boursonflure.
NANCY	(*with relish*) Boursonflure!
ANNA	I knew you'd like that. (*Hands her parcel.*) Here. Present.
NANCY	(*opening it*) You shouldn't have. (*Takes out Monopoly set.*) French Monopoly! What fun.
ANNA	I got the old version with Francs.
NANCY	Splendid.
ANNA	Remember how we used to play at school?
NANCY	We must arrange an evening before you go back with Raquel. Thank you, Annie. (*Puts it down.*) Now what do you fancy for lunch?
ANNA	Let me get it today.
NANCY	No. We agreed. (*Firmly.*) You will not do a thing while you're here.
ANNA	Well . . . all right.
	(*A knock on the door.*)
NANCY	(*calls*) Yes? Who is it?
BOUSSIRON	(*off*) C'est moi. Madame Boussiron.

NANCY   Oh lord. It's the Wicked Witch of the West. –
                 Entrez, Madame.

                 (*The door opens and* MADAME BOUSSIRON
                 *appears. She is in her 50s, very chic, dressed
                 in a beautifully cut dark suit with a scarf
                 immaculately arranged.*)

NANCY   Bonjour.

BOUSSIRON   Bonjour, Madame, Je suis désolée de vous
                 déranger mais je cherche Monsieur Charlot.

NANCY   Il est ici.

BOUSSIRON   (*tight-lipped*) Comme je le pensais.

NANCY   (*calls*) Charlot!

CHARLOT   (*comes out of shower-room*) Yes, the douche is
                 working –

                 (*He breaks off seeing* MADAME BOUSSIRON.)

BOUSSIRON   (*accusingly*) Ah, le voila!

CHARLOT   Oh. Pardon, Lydiane, mais –

BOUSSIRON   Madame, s'il vous plait. Vous m'avez promis
                 que la décoration serait terminé pour
                 aujourd'hui.

CHARLOT   Oui, je sais mais –

NANCY   C'était mon faute, Madame.

BOUSSIRON   (*corrects her*) *Ma* Faute.

NANCY   Ma faute. On a une urgence avec la douche et
                 j'ai –

BOUSSIRON   *Eu* une urgence.

NANCY	(*irritably*) Oui, eu. Et donc j'ai télephoné –
BOUSSIRON	(*cuts in*) A Monsieur Charlot. (*Pointedly.*) Qui a tout abandonné pour vous servir. (*Noticing* ANNA.) Et à qui ai-je l'honneur?
NANCY	Oh – pardon – je vous présente mon amie, Madame Carter. Elle reste avec moi.
BOUSSIRON	Enchantée, Madame.
ANNA	(*struggling*) Er – et moi – um – je suis enchantée. Aussi. Madame.
BOUSSIRON	(*sighs, to* NANCY *in near-perfect English*) I think we had better speak English.
	(NANCY *and* ANNA *exchange looks.*)
BOUSSIRON	How long have you been here, Madame?
ANNA	Nearly two weeks. I hope that's all right.
NANCY	Of course it's all right.
ANNA	I'm going back on Monday.
BOUSSIRON	However I would appreciate it, Madame Bristow, if you would inform me when you have someone staying. As specified in our agreement. I need to know who has the spare keys. A matter of security you understand.
NANCY	Yes, I'm sorry, I meant to let you know.
BOUSSIRON	And of course if the second room is occupied there is a small extra charge.
NANCY	Thank you, Madame, I am well aware of that. I will settle with you when I pay my rent.
BOUSSIRON	I will also need to verify the inventory when your friend leaves.

NANCY   I doubt she will be pinching the silverware.

BOUSSIRON   You cannot always trust people these days.
               One English tenant – titled in fact – went off
               with my cloche à fromage.

NANCY   Really? Mind you, they say our Queen Mother
               used to shoplift.

BOUSSIRON   *We* are a Republic. (*Turning to* ANNA.) I hope
               you will enjoy the rest of your stay, Madame.

ANNA   I'm sure I will. Paris is such a wonderful city.

BOUSSIRON   It is not what it was. Well I will not detain you.
               (*Sharply to* CHARLOT.) Charlot, ne trainez pas.
               Tout doit être fini aujourd'hui.

CHARLOT   (*exaggeratedly*) Oui, Madame. Bien sûr,
               Madame. (*He collects his tool kit.*)

BOUSSIRON   Aurevoir, Mesdames.

NANCY/ANNA   Aurevoir, Madame.

BOUSSIRON   (*turning back*) Oh and I will invoice you for
               the additional charge for use of the spare room.
               As specified in our agreement. (*To* CHARLOT.)
               Allons-y.

NANCY   (*aside, to* ANNA) To heel!

               (MADAME BOUSSIRON *goes out.* CHARLOT
               follows, imitating lap-dog for the benefit of
               NANCY *and* ANNA.)

NANCY   You see? What did I tell you? And the way
               Charlot runs after her like a lap-dog. (*Sighs.*)
               He needs the money of course. Actors are
               always so good at being subservient.

ANNA   (*her mind elsewhere*) However does she do it?

NANCY   What?

ANNA	Her scarf. Just so. Did you notice?
NANCY	Yes I did. And thought I'd love to throttle her with it.

(*Blackout. French song. Lights up. Evening, two days later.* NANCY, ANNA *and* RAQUEL *are sitting round the table playing Monopoly.* NANCY *is Bank and taking her job seriously.* RAQUEL *is into a second bottle of wine and already a bit tipsy.* ANNA *is beginning to wish she had never bought the game.*)

RAQUEL	(*moving her token*) Two, three, four, five. Boulevard de Cappucines. Hurray! – That's 30,000 francs.
NANCY	Thirty *two* thousand please.
RAQUEL	What?
NANCY	Boulevard de Cappucines is more expensive than the other two in the set.
ANNA	Like Bond Street in the English version.
NANCY	So that'll be two thousand more.
RAQUEL	All right! Keep your hair on.

(*She pays* NANCY *who sorts out the money carefully.*)

RAQUEL	And may I have my property?
NANCY	Hang on! Let me finish the transaction. Don't want to get my own money muddled with the Bank's. It's hard enough managing both as it is.
RAQUEL	(*to* ANNA) Nothing changes does it? She always wanted to be Bank at school, then moaned all through the game.

NANCY	I didn't want to be Bank. No one else offered. Then, as now.
ANNA	I would've, only –
NANCY	(*handing card to* RAQUEL) There you are. Boulevard de Cappucines.
RAQUEL	Thank you. (*Gleefully.*) Now all I need's the Avenue de Foch (*She pronounces it Fock.*) As the archbishop said to the actress!
NANCY	(*corrects her pointedly*). Avenue de Foch. (*Pronounced Fosh.*)
	(RAQUEL *pours herself another glass of wine.*)
NANCY	D'you think you should, Raquel?
RAQUEL	Yes I do.
NANCY	It's your liver. – Your turn, Anna.
ANNA	Sorry. Which am I? Oh yes, the iron.
	(*She shakes and moves.*)
ALL	"Allez en prison."
NANCY	Hard luck.
ANNA	I miss three goes, don't I?
NANCY	You can pay to come out if you want. 5000.
ANNA	I think I'll sit it out.
NANCY	Is that wise? Shouldn't you try to purchase more properties? Belleville won't get you far.
RAQUEL	Any more than the Old Kent Road used to. I could never understand why you always went for that, or grotty old Whitechapel.

ANNA   No one else wanted them.

NANCY   Ever the philanthropist. – So what do you want
               to do, Anna?

ANNA   Um . . . maybe I'll pay the fine and come out of
               jail.

RAQUEL   Why? You might shake a double next go and
               come out for nothing.

ANNA   Oh yes, oh dear. I'd forgotten what a
               complicated game it is. Perhaps I will stay in
               then.

NANCY   As you wish. My turn.

               (*She goes to pick up token.*)

RAQUEL   No! That's mine. I'm the racing car. You're the
               top hat.

NANCY   I know. I was only straightening it.

RAQUEL   Oh for Christ's sake!

NANCY   Well it has been known for tokens to get
               nudged into the wrong square.

RAQUEL   Nudged? Are you accusing me of cheating?

NANCY   Of course I'm not. But I do like a tidy board.

RAQUEL   "Yes, Miss. No, Miss".

NANCY   What's the matter with you this evening,
               Raquel?

RAQUEL   What do you mean?

NANCY   You seem so touchy.

RAQUEL   Touchy?

NANCY   There's nothing wrong is there?

RAQUEL   (*deliberately*) Look are you going or aren't
              you?

NANCY   (*shakes and moves*) Gare St Lazare. Mm. Might
              as well buy that.

ANNA   Three stations. That's nice.

NANCY   20,000. (*She starts to count money.*)

RAQUEL   Talking of stations, did I tell you? The other
              day, at the Gare de Nord, I was touched up by
              this creepy-looking man. He nuzzled against me
              in the ticket queue and –

NANCY   (*cuts in*) Oh that old trick. He was after your
              passport.

RAQUEL   I do know the difference between a pickpocket
              and a pervert. One picks your pocket and the
              other pockets his prick! (*She laughs slightly
              hysterically. The others don't.*) All right, it
              wasn't one of my best. (*Her mobile rings. She
              dives for it.*)

              (*with a note of desperation*) Jean-Claude? Tu
              as reçu mes textos? (*She breaks off, complete
              change of tone.*) Oh it's you . . . No, it isn't
              convenient. I'm at someone else's place . . .
              Ring me in the morning, but not till after
              eleven. I' ll be sleeping in. (*She switches off.*) It
              was only Reggie. My first husband.

ANNA   The dull one?

RAQUEL   Yes, he turns up in Paris from time to time. Still
              as dull as ditchwater.

              (*She places the mobile on the table.*)

NANCY   Would you mind switching it off please?

RAQUEL   I'm expecting an important call.

NANCY   It's hard enough to concentrate without that
                nauseating jingle interrupting every five
                minutes.

ANNA   Shall we go on? It's your turn, Raquel.

                (*She hands the dice to* RAQUEL *who shakes and
                moves.*)

RAQUEL   Chance! (*Picks up Chance card and reads it
                out.*) "La Banque vous verse un dividend de
                5000".

ANNA   Lovely.

RAQUEL   (*to* NANCY) A 5000 dividend please, Bank.

NANCY   I heard. (*She counts the money and hands it to*
                RAQUEL.) You next, Annie. Try for a double.

ANNA   (*shakes*) No. No use.

                (*She hands dice to* NANCY *who shakes and
                moves.*)

NANCY   "Avenue de Foch." Oh yes, I'll have that.

RAQUEL   (*livid*) You bet you will.

NANCY   30,000 isn't it?

RAQUEL   She's only buying it to stop me.

NANCY   That is the point of the game, dear.

ANNA   (*placatingly*) Never mind, Raquel. You've
                already got the best set. Rue de La Paix and the
                Champs Elysée.

RAQUEL   I need the Avenue de Foch.

NANCY	I might be prepared to sell it for a consideration.
RAQUEL	How much?
NANCY	Fifty thousand.
RAQUEL	You must be joking.
NANCY	Do I take it that means no?
RAQUEL	I'll give you twenty thousand.
NANCY	And have you building hotels right along that side? Not on your nelly.
RAQUEL	All right, keep the sodding thing.
NANCY	Must you resort to the language of the street?
RAQUEL	Here we go. Another lecture on swearing.
NANCY	One of the reasons I left England was the paucity of vocabulary amongst the young. And *you* haven't the excuse of youth.
RAQUEL	You were always a bitch under your head girl act.
ANNA	Oh please don't let's quarrel.
RAQUEL	It's this stupid game. It always brings out the worst in people.
NANCY	Speak for yourself, dear.
RAQUEL	And don't call me "dear", it's so bloody patronising.
ANNA	Look, if you'd sooner stop playing . . . I'd never have bought it, only I thought it would be fun.

RAQUEL   Oh and it is fun isn't it, Nancy? I'm positively full of joie de vivre.

NANCY   Cheap Beaujolais more like.

RAQUEL   Well at least I know how to let my hair down.

NANCY   By paying for extensions?

RAQUEL   I'd sooner be me than an overweight old bag whose idea of fun is an afternoon at the Musée D'Orsay OD-ing on Monet.

NANCY   You suggest I try cruising round the Bois de Bologne picking up men young enough to be my grandson.

RAQUEL   You wouldn't have a hope in hell.

NANCY   (*controlling herself*) You're right, Anna, I think we should pack up the game.

RAQUEL   Okay then, let's pack it up. As far as I'm concerned, I've had Monopoly up to here. And you, as well.

NANCY   I assure you the feeling is mutual.

           (*She starts to pack up the bank notes.*)

RAQUEL   Pompous cow.

NANCY   Drunken tart.

ANNA   Oh please, both of you –

RAQUEL   (*turning on her*) And you can shut up too, Polyanna.

NANCY   Don't you start calling *her* names.

RAQUEL   Sticking up for the little wets as usual!

NANCY   Take no notice of her Anna, she's deranged.

RAQUEL   (*getting up*) Well I think I'll get back to the
                  asylum. I prefer the company there. (*She picks
                  up the Monopoly board and hurls it on the
                  floor.*) Bonne Soirée!

                  (*She rushes out. A long horrified pause.*)

NANCY   (*eventually*) She was always a bad sport.

ANNA   Raymond was the same.

NANCY   (*still seething*) She is the *end*.

ANNA   We'd better clean up.

NANCY   Probably had a tiff with the toy boy.

                  (ANNA *goes to pick up the pieces.*)

                  Oh leave that, Anna.

                  (*The mobile lets out its horrid jingle.*)

                  God, not that.

                  (*She picks it up and tries to stop it.*)

                  Damn thing. How do you stop it?

ANNA   I don't know.

NANCY   (*to mobile*) Oh shut up. (*Shakes it.*) I've half a
                  mind to flush it down the loo.

ANNA   Give it to me. I'll go after her. She can't have
                  got far, not in those heels.

NANCY   No, I'll take it. And give her a bit of my mind
                  while I'm about it.

ANNA   (*as* NANCY *makes for the door*) Do you think
                  that's wise?

NANCY   (*hurrying out*) I don't care. (*Off, on stairs.*)
         Raquel! Raquel! (*Further off.*) Are you down
         there? – Come back and answer your bloody
         mobile before I –

         (*She breaks off with a cry. Then a crash as she
         falls. The mobile stops its jingle.*)

ANNA   Nancy? (*Pause, then anxiously.*) Nancy!

         (*As she hurries out the horrid jingle starts
         again. The sound rises as the curtain falls.*)

ACT TWO

Scene One

A week later. NANCY *is sitting with her leg up on a footstool, her ankle is in a large hospital boot, wrist bandaged. Nearby is a walking stick. She is fed up.*

After a moment she straightens her spine and endeavours to compose her body and mind ready for meditation. She joins her palms together with difficulty, wincing as she does so. She starts to breathe yoga-style.

NANCY   (*chanting her mantra*) Bugger, bugger, bugger.

                (*She gives up. Pause. She sees book on table, gets up with difficulty, unable to put weight on ankle or wrist. She reaches for the stick and knocks it over. Growls with frustration as* ANNA *comes in carrying shopping. Their roles have changed.* ANNA *is now in charge.*)

ANNA   Nancy! I told you not to move until I got back.

NANCY   I was only trying to reach –

ANNA   (*continues over*) Do you want to end up in hospital again?

NANCY   No but –

ANNA   Then sit down.

                (*She puts shopping down and goes to help her.*)

NANCY   Nor do I want a nursemaid fussing over me.

ANNA   I know, but you must take care.

NANCY   Sorry. (*As* ANNA *helps her to sit.*) I just feel so useless.

(ANNA *lifts her leg back onto foot stool.*)

NANCY   You were the one who was meant to be spoilt.

(ANNA *puts cushion at her back.*)

NANCY   You come to Paris for a holiday and end up
                 dressing me, feeding me, potting me.

ANNA   Now stop that.

                 (*She unpacks the shopping during the
                 following.*)

NANCY   Twenty years looking after an invalid husband
                 and now you're stuck with *me*.

ANNA   I don't think a fractured fibula is a terminal
                 condition. Nor a sprained wrist.

NANCY   If they were I'd take matters into my own
                 hands.

ANNA   Oh Nancy.

NANCY   I would. I've got it all taped. Good supply of
                 pills, bottle of cognac and Bob's your uncle.

ANNA   I believe it's advisable to put a plastic bag over
                 your head as well.

NANCY   I don't call that dying with dignity.

ANNA   Rather depends if it's Fortnums or Tescos.

NANCY   Printemps or Intermarché.

                 (*They laugh.*)

NANCY   Anyway they're banning plastic bags now.

ANNA   They say a bath does the trick too. You take
                 the pills, swill down the drink then lie back in a
                 bathful of Radox.

NANCY   And drift into oblivion.

ANNA   No, die of hypothermia. Eventually.

NANCY   Perhaps I'll just hang myself. I knew someone,
               an old colleague. She'd had several strokes.
               Dragged herself to the bedroom window and
               threw herself out.

ANNA   What a way to go.

NANCY   She didn't go. Just cracked her head on a
               flowerpot.

               (*They laugh hysterically.*)

ANNA   We shouldn't laugh.

NANCY   Why not? Let's face it, God must have a sense
               of humour. Albeit a somewhat warped one.

               (*A pause.*)

NANCY   Did Raymond ever consider . . . ?

ANNA   (*with sudden bitterness*) And let me off the
               hook? Not likely. (*A beat.*) Want a coffee?

NANCY   Please.

               (ANNA *goes to make coffee.* NANCY *looks at
               her, realising the full extent of her feelings.*)

NANCY   Why didn't you leave him, Annie?

               (*A pause as* ANNA *debates whether to tell her
               or not.*)

ANNA   I nearly did once. Years ago. Before he became
               ill. I was so . . . lonely.

NANCY   Why didn't you get a job?

ANNA	Raymond didn't approve of women working.
NANCY	(*a grunt of disapproval*) Huh.
ANNA	I know I should've pulled my finger out. Gone to adult education classes, found voluntary work, the sort of things other women did. But I felt so . . . inadequate. Perhaps if we'd had children . . .
NANCY	Yes.
ANNA	And then I met someone. He worked in the local library. We discussed books sometimes. That was all. To begin with. I mean you can't really . . .
NANCY	Proposition someone in a silent reading room.
ANNA	But we both *knew*.
NANCY	"And from her eyes I did receive fair speechless messages."
ANNA	Then one day I met him in the park. It was his lunch hour. He was sitting on a bench eating his sandwiches. Cheese and pickle. He shared them with me, and we talked about – everything. As if we'd known each other for years. He wasn't only a librarian. He wrote short stories.
NANCY	(*impressed*) Really?
ANNA	For womens' magazines.
NANCY	Oh.
ANNA	He was a great favourite with "People's Friend." He liked happy endings.
NANCY	What was his name?
ANNA	Cressida Lovejoy.

NANCY	A pseudonym I trust.
ANNA	His real name was David. Anyway, after that we met regularly.
NANCY	And graduated from cheese and pickle to smoked salmon.
ANNA	Coronation chicken actually. One thing led to another.
NANCY	Or as Raquel would say, "*the* other."
ANNA	There wasn't much of that. None really. We did spend one wonderful afternoon together. He took the day off. We drove into the country, went for a walk in a wood. We found a little clearing near a stream. There were bluebells and birds singing –
NANCY	Sounds like one of his romantic stories.
ANNA	No, it was total disaster. Have you ever tried making love on a bed of pine needles?
NANCY	Can't say I have.
ANNA	Then it started to rain. We rushed back to the car. But that was even worse. (*Smiling at the memory.*) He nearly punctured his spleen on the gear lever, and I half strangled myself with the safety belt. God, how we laughed. Raymond never had a sense of humour.
NANCY	Mm, I remember his speech at your wedding.
ANNA	I'd forgotten what it was like to laugh. It was that decided me.
NANCY	To leave him?
ANNA	I could've left a note, but it seemed only fair to tell him face to face.

NANCY   How did he react?

ANNA   It was dreadful.

NANCY   He didn't beat you up?

ANNA   That might've been better. He just looked at me
           scathingly and said, "The poor man must be
           mentally deficient."

NANCY   Bastard.

ANNA   I told him I was going. Later that evening he
           had his first heart attack.

NANCY   No.

ANNA   I couldn't leave him after that. He said it was
           my fault.

NANCY   Rubbish.

ANNA   It might've been. I mean . . . the shock. I felt so
           guilty.

NANCY   So you spent the next twenty years being
           emotionally blackmailed.

ANNA   I didn't know it would go on all that time. He
           was quite a bit older than me. And then when
           MS was diagnosed too . . . he seemed so
           helpless. And he wouldn't have carers in.

NANCY   I bet he wouldn't.

ANNA   The doctor said it was *me* that kept him going. I
           suppose it was in a way – his loathing of me.

NANCY   Oh Annie.

ANNA   He simply wouldn't let go.

NANCY   What happened to your librarian?

ANNA   I tried to . . . explain . . . but it was so . . . Later
                I heard he'd transferred to another branch. I
                bought People's Friend for a while, hoping I'd
                see one of his stories. But I never did.

NANCY   Perhaps he gave up on happy endings.

ANNA   I hope not. (*Changing subject.*) Hey, I got us
                another crossword book. Or rather "Mots
                Croisés." (*Putting it beside her.*) Level
                "Simple."

NANCY   We should be expert by the time I'm out of
                here.

                (*Doorbell rings.*)

NANCY   (*groans*) Don't let that be Madame Boussiron. I
                should've been touch with her.

                (ANNA *goes to the door and opens it. It is*
                CHARLOT *with a bouquet of flowers.*)

ANNA   (*her face lighting up*) Charlot!

CHARLOT   Bonjour!

NANCY   Thank God.

CHARLOT   (*proferring flowers*) For you, Mesdames.

NANCY   How sweet of you.

ANNA   They're beautiful.

NANCY   Thank you, Charlot.

ANNA   I'll put them in water.

                (*She moves off to kitchen area and puts them
                in vase during the following.*)

CHARLOT   (*to* NANCY)And how is the "damaged" soldier
             today. Or should it be "injured" soldier?

NANCY   Wounded actually.

CHARLOT   Wounded. – Hurt. A toi, Nancy.

NANCY   Damaged, injured, wounded, what's the
             difference? They all amount to the same bloody
             thing. *Me* imprisoned here for another month.

CHARLOT   Come on, be a sport. Wounded. Hurt. – Your
             turn.

NANCY   I'm not in the mood.

             (*As* ANNA *returns with the flowers.*)

CHARLOT   Well I have news to cheer you up. I have been
             hired to do a one-man show, starting in two
             weeks.

ANNA   Oh that's wonderful, Charlot.

NANCY   Yes, congratulations. Where's it to be held?

CHARLOT   Not the Olympia I'm afraid. A bar in St Denis.
             But my agent is bringing some producers
             along.

ANNA   Splendid.

CHARLOT   And you are both invited as my guests. You
             can go by taxi.

NANCY   And how, pray, am I supposed to get down six
             flights?

CHARLOT   All that is arranged. My friend Rocco – who is
             an ex-wrestler – will help me to carry you down
             the stairs.

NANCY   Don't be so ridiculous. I'd end up with a
             broken neck too. And you'd both be flattened.

ANNA	She's right. We couldn't take the risk. She must rest that ankle.
NANCY	But Anna can go.
CHARLOT	I hope, yes.
ANNA	It's very kind of you Charlot, but I can't leave Nancy –
NANCY	(*cuts in*) For heaven's sake. I'm not Raymond. I can cope on my own for one evening.
ANNA	Oh yes! I know you. You'd be taking all sorts of stupid risks.
NANCY	Then we'll get a babysitter. (*To* CHARLOT.) Perhaps your friend Rocco would oblige. Does he do nappy-changing as well as half Nelsons?
CHARLOT	(*doubtful*) I could ask him . . .
	(NANCY *and* ANNA *burst out laughing.*)
	Ah, the English sense of humour.
	(*He joins in their laughter.*)
NANCY	Oh lord – shouldn't laugh –
ANNA	Do you want to . . . ?
NANCY	Please. (*To* CHARLOT, *as* ANNA *helps her up.*) Nature calls.
CHARLOT	The "auntie"?
NANCY	(*trying not to laugh*) Stop it.
ANNA	(*to* CHARLOT, *as they go into bathroom*) We'll be back in a minute. Can you put the coffee on?

(*She closes the bathroom door. Pause.*
CHARLOT *goes to see to coffee. After a moment*
ANNA *comes out of bathroom.*)

ANNA   (*to* NANCY) Call me when you're ready. (*She
        closes door.*) She won't be long.

CHARLOT   She is not so fine.

ANNA   She is physically. The fracture should be
        healed in a few weeks.

CHARLOT   The problem is in her head?

ANNA   She's used to being in charge. She hates
        relying on other people.

CHARLOT   She is lucky to have you.

ANNA   It's been a good excuse for me to stay on here.

CHARLOT   Every cloud has the silver lining. – I am happy
        you are staying. And happy you are coming to
        my show.

ANNA   I can't promise, Charlot. I shall have to see how
        things go.

CHARLOT   Please. After all it is for you I have created the
        programme.

ANNA   Me?

CHARLOT   Yes. Well you and Nancy.

ANNA   What's it about then?

CHARLOT   It's a melange – mixture – of songs of the 50s
        and 60s. All your old favourites.

ANNA   How lovely. It'll be packed out. All the English
        women in Paris will be coming.

CHARLOT   There is only one I wish to be there.

ANNA   Stop flirting, Charlot.

CHARLOT   With you I do not flirt. I mean it.

                (*His mobile rings.*)

CHARLOT   Meurt. Excuse me. (*On phone.*) Bonjour . . . Oh
                c'est toi, Lydiane. – Ce n'est pas tout a fait le
                moment . . . Tu dis urgent? Quel est le problem?
                . . . Ah. – Entendu . . . Oui, j'arrive des que
                possible. (*Switches off, turns to* ANNA.)
                Lydiane. Er – Madame Boussiron.

ANNA   Another summons?

CHARLOT   Emergency. A leaking ceiling.

ANNA   You'd better go then.

CHARLOT   You will come won't you? To my show?

ANNA   I'll try.

CHARLOT   Au revoir.

                (*He kisses her on each cheek, then looks at
                her for a moment.*)

CHARLOT   You are beautiful. – And that is not flirting
                either.

NANCY   (*off*) Annie! Ready!

CHARLOT   A bientôt.

                (*He goes.* ANNA *looks after him.*)

NANCY   (*off*) Annie!

ANNA   Coming.

(*She hurries towards the bathroom. Blackout. French song. Then lights up. Evening. A few days later.*)

(NANCY *is sitting with her leg up wishing that her visitor,* RAQUEL, *would go.* RAQUEL *is listless and subdued, her hair in need of a cut and tint, no longer dressed to kill. A pause.* RAQUEL *looks surreptitiously at her watch.* NANCY *notices, then starts doing leg exercises. Another pause.*)

NANCY   You really don't have to stay, Raquel.

RAQUEL   I wish you'd stop saying that.

NANCY   I'm sure you've better things to do.

RAQUEL   I promised Annie I'd wait till she got back.

NANCY   (*edgy*) I don't need a babysitter. Sorry, that was churlish. It was sweet of you to come, but . . .

RAQUEL   'Least I could do. It was all my fault. You doing your ankle, and –

NANCY   Nonsense.

RAQUEL   If I hadn't left my bloody cell-phone behind.

NANCY   If I hadn't taken the stairs three at a time. Anyway it's all past history now. So if there's somewhere you'd rather be . . .

RAQUEL   (*edgy*) There isn't, thank you.

(*Pause.* NANCY *gives her a look.*)

RAQUEL   How long does this soirée of Charlot's go on?

NANCY   Should be over by now. But they'll probably stay for a drink after.

RAQUEL   They'll need it if it's anything like the last one.
            Is it another of his anti-war wanks?

NANCY   No. Songs of the past and some of his own
            compositions.

RAQUEL   Oh gawd.

NANCY   Sure you won't have a glass of wine?

RAQUEL   No thanks. I'm de-toxing. That's why I'm such
            scintillating company.

NANCY   Join the club. I'm so fed up with being stuck
            here. If only there was a lift. At least I could
            hobble along to the patisserie.

            (*Pause.*)

RAQUEL   Shall we play a game?

NANCY   What do you suggest? Monopoly?

RAQUEL   Maybe not.

            (*They laugh, in spite of themselves, at the
            memory.*)

NANCY   That reminds me we still haven't found the top
            hat.

RAQUEL   I'll buy you another set.

NANCY   (*peevishly*) I don't want another set. I want my
            top hat.

RAQUEL   Shall I have a look for it?

NANCY   No. Annie's looked everywhere.

            (*Pause.*)

RAQUEL   That was a bloody awful evening.

NANCY	I've known better.
RAQUEL	I was in a foul mood.
NANCY	A trifle tetchy.
RAQUEL	It wasn't just the Avenue Foch set me off.
NANCY	. . . Jean-Claude?
RAQUEL	Yes. He'd just ditched me.
NANCY	I'm sorry, Raquel.
RAQUEL	Don't be. I'm well rid of the little turd. Young men may be tasty, but they don't give a damn about anyone but themselves. Always looking over your shoulder at their own reflexion, preening in shop windows. Can't even have a decent conversation with them. They're permanently plugged into their i-pods . . . Next time I'm going for an older man. Of at least forty.
NANCY	Have you ever thought of taking a break?
RAQUEL	How do you mean?
NANCY	Doing without them.
RAQUEL	*Men?*
NANCY	Your track record isn't exactly auspicious. Perhaps if you tried something else . . .
RAQUEL	(*suspiciously*) Like what?
NANCY	Celibacy?
RAQUEL	Oh. For a moment I thought you were propositioning me.
NANCY	Do you mind!

RAQUEL   You know I used to think you were that way
            inclined. Didn't you live with another woman?

NANCY   For fifteen years, But neither of us were "that
            way inclined." We were just friends. I don't
            know why I say "just." There's no better thing
            than true friendship. We were companions. We
            read the same books, did crosswords together,
            walked at the same pace. Shared silences. She
            died two years ago. Coronary. Another reason I
            came to Paris.

RAQUEL   I've never had a close friend. Only lovers.

NANCY   Friends you choose. Lovers are a matter of
            estrogen.

RAQUEL   Can't you have both?

NANCY   Only if you're very lucky.

RAQUEL   I can't imagine being celibate.

NANCY   They say it's only when you're having sex
            regularly it seems essential. When you stop,
            you fill your life with a myriad other things and
            you wonder how you ever fitted it in.

RAQUEL   As the archbishop said to the actress.
            (*Laughs.*)

NANCY   Oh, back on form I see! – Anyway I don't know
            how people have the energy at our age.

RAQUEL   A combination of vanity and vitamins.

NANCY   Perhaps if you hadn't changed your name. I
            mean a name like Raquel takes some living up
            to. Why did you change it, and when?

RAQUEL   "One Million Years Before Christ."

NANCY   What?

RAQUEL   Raquel Welch.

NANCY   Oh I remember. Plastered over the underground in a fur bikini.

RAQUEL   And all the men drooling over her. Why not me, I thought So I dumped dreary little Rachel, had my teeth fixed, dyed my hair, bought a padded bra –

NANCY   And never looked back.

RAQUEL   Until now . . . You and Annie turning up here, shades of the past . . .

NANCY   I rather liked Rachel.

RAQUEL   So did Reggie. She was almost as dull as him.

            (*Sound of voices and laughter off on the stairs.*)

NANCY   Sounds as if they're back.

RAQUEL   And in high spirits. It's good to see Annie enjoying herself.

NANCY   Yes . . .

            (*Door opens as* ANNA *and* CHARLOT *come in. He is carrying a guitar. General greetings.*)

NANCY   (*to* CHARLOT) How did the show go?

CHARLOT   Not so bad.

ANNA   He was terrific.

CHARLOT   I wouldn't say so.

ANNA   Don't be modest. (*To* NANCY/RAQUEL, *concernedly.*) Was everything all right here?

RAQUEL   No, disaster. She passed out cold and I had to
            give her the kiss of life.

NANCY   Idiot!

ANNA   I wish you could've come too. You'd have
            loved it. He sang all the old songs.

RAQUEL   I never knew you sang, Charlot.

CHARLOT   Not sing, exactly. I just . . . (*He looks at* ANNA.)
            . . . "put over the numbers."

ANNA   Right.

NANCY   Like Maurice Chevalier.

CHARLOT   Not quite.

ANNA   He sang all our favourites. And some of his
            own things too.

RAQUEL   You compose as well?

CHARLOT   I try.

ANNA   On the way home he made up a song, for *us*.

CHARLOT   "Les Dames Anglaises."

ANNA   (*laughing at the memory*) We nearly got
            thrown off the Metro.

RAQUEL   Oh can we hear it?

NANCY   Yes, we could do with some light
            entertainment.

CHARLOT   It is not yet finished. There are holes still.

ANNA   Go on, Charlot.

            (*They urge him on.*)

CHARLOT   If you insist. – I shall need some help.

                   (*He takes his guitar and sits down.*)

CHARLOT   (*twangs guitar*)
                   If they are finding life is drear
                   In Harrogate or Haslemere
                   And need a bit of ooh-la-la,
                   They just jump on the Eurostar.

                   (*sings*)
                   Les Dames Anglaises, les Dames Anglaises,
                   You see them everywhere these days,
                   Clutching guides and Pariscopes,
                   Making sure they know the ropes.
                   Les Dames Anglaises, les Dames Anglaises.
                   I wonder is it just a craze?
                   Will they vanish in a haze?
                   What is it that casts such a spell?
                   Surely not the Tour Eiffel.

                   (*The women laugh.*)

CHARLOT   Now I am a bit stuck. – Tell me, ladies, why do
                   you come to Paris?

                   (*He points to each in turn.*)

CHARLOT   Nancy –

NANCY   To see the Impressionists.

CHARLOT   Raquel –

RAQUEL   To have my handies kissed.

CHARLOT   Anna –

ANNA   To find what I have missed.

CHARLOT   Bravo! (*Sings.*)
                   Les Dames Anglaises, les Dames Anglaises.
                   You see them everywhere these days.
                   All of different shapes and sizes,

Casting off their cares and crises.
Les Dames Anglaises, les Dames Anglaises,
Strolling on the Champs Elysée,
Meeting in salons de thé –é,

(*The women groan.*)

Off to conversation class,
To tell their elbow from their ar– (*Hastily.*)

(*Pointing to them again.*)

Alors, ladies! Why else do you come to Paris?

(*Pointing at them again.*)

NANCY   To study Jean-Paul Sartre.

RAQUEL   To lose my bleeding heart-re.

ANNA   To live life à-la-carte.

(*They all laugh, and as* CHARLOT *continues,*
RAQUEL *grabs* ANNA *and they waltz as* NANCY
beats time with her walking stick.)

CHARLOT   (*sings*)
Les Dames Anglaises, Les Dames Anglaises.
You see them everywhere these days,
Cruising on the bateaux mouches,
Wrestling with a dodgy douche.

(*They laugh and continue on not hearing the
door which opens. It is* MADAME BOUSSIRON.)

CHARLOT   Les Dames Anglaises, les Dames Anglaises,
You see them everywhere these days,
Dining in the Deux Magots,
Dancing in the . . .

BOUSSIRON   Quiet, please!

(CHARLOT *peters out as he sees* BOUSSIRON. *The
others freeze*).

NANCY	Madame, Bonsoir. Do come in.
BOUSSIRON	(*through gritted teeth*) I have been knocking on the door for at least five minutes.
NANCY	We didn't hear you.
BOUSSIRON	I am not surprised.
NANCY	Oh dear. Were we making a bit of a din?
BOUSSIRON	I could hear you from the street.
RAQUEL	Quel horreur!
BOUSSIRON	Some of your neighbours are trying to sleep.
NANCY	I'm so sorry.
BOUSSIRON	It clearly states in our agreement that there should be no disturbances after 23.00 hours.
NANCY	Oh lord, is that the time? We didn't realise.
RAQUEL	Charlot was serenading us.
CHARLOT	Yes, it was my fault.
ANNA	(*stepping forward*) No, it wasn't, Charlot. (*To* BOUSSIRON.) He very kindly brought me home after his show and –
BOUSSIRON	(*feigning surprise*) Madame Carter! I thought you had returned to England.
ANNA	Only for a couple of days while Nancy was in hospital. I had to collect more clothes.
NANCY	She's staying on to look after me. I had a rather nasty fall.
RAQUEL	Took a header down your stairs.

BOUSSIRON	Why was I not informed?
RAQUEL	Oh for Pete's sake.
NANCY	I had every intention of doing so but, as you can see, I have been somewhat hors de combat. (*Aside*.) And thank you for your sympathy.
BOUSSIRON	Then Charlot should have told me. He seems to spend most of his time here.
NANCY	Yes, I don't know what I'd have done without him.
ANNA	He's been an absolute angel.
CHARLOT	It was nothing.
BOUSSIRON	(*to* CHARLOT) Pourquoi tu ne me pas dit qu'elle est encore ici?
CHARLOT	Desolé mais, je pensais que –
NANCY	It isn't Charlot's job to carry messages.
BOUSSIRON	But it is his job to entertain you at this hour?
RAQUEL	Oh come on, sweetie, it's no big deal.
NANCY	He was only trying to cheer me up.
RAQUEL	(*muting it*) He's written a song for us. In praise of English Women.
BOUSSIRON	(*seething*) Has he?
ANNA	(*smiling at* CHARLOT) "Les Dames Anglaises."
RAQUEL	Perhaps Madame would like to hear it.
CHARLOT	(*hastily*) I don't think so, Raquel.
NANCY	Maybe she doesn't share his admiration for the English.

BOUSSIRON   Frankly I do not.

RAQUEL   Now she tells us.

BOUSSIRON   In future I shall let my flats only to the
                 Japanese.

RAQUEL   Bully for them.

BOUSSIRON   They are excellent tenants. Considerate, quiet
                 and clean.

NANCY   (*indignantly*) Are you suggesting we're not
                 clean?

RAQUEL   That's ripe coming from a frog.

BOUSSIRON   (*fuming*) How dare you? Oh the Channel
                 Tunnel has a lot to answer for. You people!
                 You come over here with your atrocious
                 accents and *Daily Mails* and dreadful sandals –

NANCY   (*indignant*) I never read the *Daily Mail*.

BOUSSIRON   You have ruined this city.

NANCY   I'd say you'd done pretty well out of the
                 English.

BOUSSIRON   (*in full flood now*) What have you brought to
                 us?

RAQUEL   Fat rents for a start.

BOUSSIRON   Nothing but fish and chips and Mad Cow
                 Disease.

RAQUEL.   You're the mad cow.

BOUSSIRON   Salope! (*Bitch.*)

CHARLOT   Lydiane –

BOUSSIRON	(*turning on* CHARLOT) Ne to mêle pas de ça!
ANNA	(*pacifyingly*) Look can't we just calm down and –
NANCY	No, Anna, let her get it out of her system.
BOUSSIRON	Not content to ruin our cities, you must ruin our countryside, too. You buy our houses so we cannot afford to live in our own villages, you push yourselves on to our parish councils. There is even an English mayor in the Dardogne.
RAQUEL	You should count yourselves lucky.
BOUSSIRON	You turn our bistros into pubs and replace our cafés with Starbucks.
ANNA	Actually Starbucks is American.
BOUSSIRON	English, American, it is the same thing.
NANCY	Now *that* I do object to.
BOUSSIRON	You are both war-mongers. Look at Iraq.
NANCY	So are the French when it suits them.
BOUSSIRON	*We* fight for our principles, not just for oil.
NANCY	Principles? The French? What about Vichy? And where would you be if we hadn't seen off the Germans in World War Two?
RAQUEL	God, they'll be raking up Agincourt next.
CHARLOT	"Once more unto the breach, dear friends, once more!"
BOUSSIRON	Tais-toi! (*To the women.*) Yes, your Shakespeare made a cheap romance of Agincourt.

NANCY

Are you calling Henry the Fifth a cheap romance?

ANNA

(*suddenly forceful*) Please! Stop it! All of you.

BOUSSIRON

(*to* ANNA) This is not your business.

CHARLOT

No, she is right, Lydiane.

BOUSSIRON

(*to* CHARLOT) Vas-y, prends sa defence! Je vole bien de quel côtè tu es.

NANCY

(*with difficulty*) Very well then. Let's call a truce.

RAQUEL.

Oh why? I was rather enjoying it.

NANCY

I think we've had enough for one night.

BOUSSIRON

Certainly I have had enough. (*To* NANCY.) Madame Bristow, you will vacate this appartment by the end of the month.

ANNA

No!

NANCY

You can't do that.

BOUSSIRON

Yes I can. The agreement clearly states –

RAQUEL

Fuck the agreement.

BOUSSIRON

(*to* RAQUEL) And you will leave your appartment too, Madame. You will both receive your notice in writing tomorrow. (*Gathering her dignity.*) Meanwhile I wish you good night. (*She turns to* CHARLOT.) Viens, Charlot.

(CHARLOT *hesitates, then holds his ground.*)

BOUSSIRON

Allez, viens!

CHARLOT

(*looks at* ANNA, *then, in English*) No. I am staying.

RAQUEL   Bravo.

BOUSSIRON   (*shocked*) Je comprends . . . As you wish. (*She
                turns to* ANNA.) But don't think you will have
                much luck with him, Madame. He cannot even
                get it up.

                (*She goes. A stunned pause.*)

NANCY   Well . . . she certainly has a good grasp of the
                idiom.

                (RAQUEL *and* NANCY *start to laugh
                hysterically.* CHARLOT *looks unhappily
                towards* ANNA *who stands still, shaken.*)

RAQUEL   Bring on the Japanese!

                (*She starts to sing as the lights dim.*)

                Les Japonaises, they have their ways,
                They meditate for days and days –

                (*Blackout. Lights up. Later the same evening.*
                CHARLOT *is sitting head in hands. Intermittent
                voices off in* NANCY'S *room. A pause, then the
                bedroom door opens as* ANNA *comes out.*)

ANNA   (*to* NANCY) Goodnight, sleep well. And don't
                worry, we'll sort everything out.

                (*She closes the door and turns into room.
                Pulls up as she sees* CHARLOT. *He gets up.*)

                I thought you had gone.

CHARLOT   I want to talk to you.

ANNA   It's very late, Charlot.

CHARLOT   Five minutes only. Please.

ANNA   (*beat*) All right.

(She sits down.)

CHARLOT   *(embarrassed)* What Lydiane said about me –
            that – well . . . that I –

(He gestures with his hands.)

ANNA   *(tightly, misconstruing)* I'm not interested in
            your sexual prowess, Charlot.

CHARLOT   No, no, I didn't mean – I meant – what she
            thought about you and me – us – that we are
            having a relation.

ANNA   It doesn't matter what she thinks.

CHARLOT   Yes it does.

ANNA   *We* know there is nothing between us.

CHARLOT   But there is. You are my – deep friend.

ANNA   Who will be going back to England as soon as
            Nancy can manage on her own.

CHARLOT   I don't want that you think bad of me.

ANNA   I don't. Your private life is no concern of mine.

CHARLOT   But I have to explain. I want no deceptions
            with you. *(With difficulty.)* After Cheryl and
            Lottie left me, I was so . . . empty. I started
            playing the fields. I had several liaisons.

ANNA   Including Madame Boussiron.

CHARLOT   But it meant nothing.

ANNA   It obviously did to her.

CHARLOT   Yes. I am ashamed for that. I have made use of
            her. I needed money to send for Lottie, Lydiane
            offered me the part-time jobs with her tenants. I

couldn't afford to turn her down so . . . (*He trails off.*)

ANNA   (*cuttingly*) You serviced her too.

CHARLOT   Only for a short time. You must believe me, Anna. It is ages since I had the leg over.

(ANNA *smothers a laugh.*)

CHARLOT   "Leg over" is wrong?

ANNA   There are more delicate ways of putting it.

CHARLOT   How would you say it?

ANNA   . . . Making love.

CHARLOT   But it wasn't "making love." I had no love for her. That is why she is jealous of you and why she is saying those things. – You *did* mind what she said?

ANNA   Of course I did.

CHARLOT   So you do like me a little bit?

ANNA   You know I do, but . . .

CHARLOT   You do not fancy me?

ANNA   I am sixty five, Charlot.

CHARLOT   So? Age doesn't matter. Look at Raquel.

ANNA   I'm not Raquel. (*Gently.*) I'd like us to remain what you said – "deep friends."

CHARLOT   (*shrugs with assumed nonchalance*) Okay. You can't be winning them all.

ANNA   Don't be like that. And please don't be hurt. – I have so much to thank you for, Charlot. For showing me Paris, for making me laugh, for

reminding me what it is to have fun. I shall
never forget riding on the back of your
motorbike round the Bois de Bologne! And for
making me feel good about myself again.
(*Thinking of her librarian.*) That's something
I haven't felt for a very long time.

CHARLOT   I thank you too.

ANNA   For what?

CHARLOT   For caring. It was so good tonight to know
there was someone there who really wanted
that I was a success, and not just for the ten
percent. And the words you said to me
afterwards

ANNA   I meant them.

CHARLOT   I know you did. I could see in your eyes. They
weren't just the kind clichés everyone says to
actors after a show. I was singing the songs for
you, Anna.

ANNA   (*lightly*) And I thought you were trying to
impress that producer.

CHARLOT   Him too!

(*They share a smile.*)

ANNA   And you obviously did. He said he'd be in
touch.

CHARLOT   People say things. He'll probably forget.

ANNA   Don't be such a pessimist. You must have faith
in yourself.

CHARLOT   . . . He is casting a new show. It will tour first
and then be playing a season in Paris. If I had a
part in it I could save money. And perhaps
Lottie will be proud of me.

ANNA   That's what really matters to you, isn't it?
            Lottie.

CHARLOT   When she was born, it was the best moment of
            my life. I should have battled more hard for my
            rights as her father but I had no . . .

ANNA   Self-esteem?

CHARLOT   No courage. Like those fathers in England who
            sit on top of Buckingham Palace and drop paint
            in your House of Parliament. If I'd had "guts" I
            would have . . . I don't know . . .

ANNA   Squatted in the Elysée Palace?

CHARLOT   Or challenged Chuck to a duel.

ANNA   It's not too late.

CHARLOT   He'd probably win.

ANNA   I don't mean you should fight him. I think
            you'd have more chance just being yourself.

CHARLOT   You give me courage.

ANNA   (*a beat*) Friends then?

CHARLOT   Yes. – A toi. Friends.

ANNA   Companions.

CHARLOT   Camarades. (*Corrects himself.*) Comrades.

ANNA   Pals.

CHARLOT   Chums.

ANNA   Allies.

CHARLOT   That terrible thing Chuck says. Buddies.

ANNA   Muckers.

CHARLOT   Loved ones.

ANNA   Soul-mates.

CHARLOT   . . . You are all those things. (*As she smiles.*)
And you no longer cover your mouth when you
smile.

ANNA   I've you to thank for that, too.

CHARLOT   (*beat*) I don't want you to leave Paris.

ANNA   I hope you'll come and visit me visit me one
day.

CHARLOT   In Norfolk?

ANNA   If I'm still there. I may move. I've put the house
on the market.

CHARLOT   Your Noel Coward, he says it is, "very flat,
Norfolk."

ANNA   It is . . .

CHARLOT   Why not try Eastbourne?

ANNA   (*laughs*) I think you've romanticised
Eastbourne just as Nancy and I did Paris.

CHARLOT   The rose-coloured spectacles.

ANNA   La Vie en Rose.

CHARLOT   I suppose. – I had better go now. I say
goodnight.

ANNA   Not night. It's almost morning. (*Moving to the
window.*) Look, the sun's rising over Notre
Dame.

(CHARLOT *joins her at the window. He puts his arm round her as they look out, in a relaxed companionable way. Curtain.*)

Scene Two

A month later.

Bags and cases packed, ready to go. Some clothes laid over the back of the sofa. The flat clean and tidy.

NANCY *comes in from the bedroom. She is now dressed in her conservative headmistress gear. Although she is no longer bandaged she walks warily, conscious of her ankle. She stands for a moment looking round the room nostalgically, then she moves to the window for a last look out at the view.*

After a moment ANNA *comes out of the attic room carrying her hand luggage.*

ANNA	(*from stairs*) I think that's all. (*Seeing* NANCY.) Oh, back in headmistress mode.
NANCY	Trying to acclimatise. (*A last look around.*) A year, and I've taken all this for granted. Tomorrow I'll look out of my window in Haslemere and it'll seem as if I'd never been away.
ANNA	No, you'll always have Paris with you. I know I shall, and I've only been here two months. –
NANCY	I wish it hadn't had to end like this. (*Briskly.*) When's Charlot due?
ANNA	In about twenty minutes. He's coming straight from rehearsal.
NANCY	I'm so glad he got that job.
ANNA	Yes. A long tour is just what he needs.
NANCY	He's going to miss you.

ANNA   And you.

NANCY   Les Dames Anglaises. (*Pause.*) Well we might
            as well sit down.

            (*She walks carefully to the armchair, as she
            sits she turns away fighting back a sob.*)

NANCY   Damn –

            (ANNA *goes to her.*)

            Don't take any notice.

            (*She feels for a handkerchief without success.
            ANNA hands her hers. NANCY blows her nose.*)

ANNA   It's bound to be upsetting.

NANCY   It's not . . . just – going. It's knowing I'll never
            again be able to do anything without being
            careful. I shan't be able to run up the stairs
            or dance spontaneously.

ANNA   The doctor said you'll be fine.

NANCY   So long as I "go easy." Go easy! I've never
            gone easy in my life. (*Beat.*) I suddenly feel so
            old.

ANNA   You'll soon snap out of it.

NANCY   That's what I'm afraid of.

            (*They laugh in spite of themselves.*)

NANCY   You'll be telling me next that I'll bounce back.

ANNA   You will. – What's "bounce" in French?

NANCY   Rebondir? Or is that for a ball? "Sauter"
            perhaps. Not that it matters any more.

ANNA   Oh you must keep your French up, Nancy.

NANCY   You mean start a Cercle Francais de Haslemere?

ANNA   You'll be back here on visits.

NANCY   It won't be the same. Staying in some package
            hotel where all the staff want to practise their
            English, and they palm you off with
            yesterday's croissants.

            (*The phone rings*.)

ANNA   I'll get it. (*Answers phone*.) Bonjour. Le
            residence de Madame Bristow.

NANCY   Not for much longer.

ANNA   (*on phone*) It's me speaking . . . Oh hello, Mr
            Vane . . . No! Really? – Yes, yes it is . . . Oh I
            see . . . Yes it does . . . Yes I will. Certainly. –
            Look, I'll be back in England tomorrow. Can we
            discuss it then? Fine . . . Thank you for letting
            me know . . . Goodbye.

            (*She hangs up*.)

ANNA   Would you believe it? There's been an offer on
            my house.

NANCY   Already?

ANNA   I know! I thought it'd be on the market forever.

NANCY   Someone obviously wants it.

ANNA   Yes. For an open prison.

NANCY   You're joking.

ANNA   No. Raymond would turn in his grave.

NANCY   Wasn't it a prison already?

ANNA

I'm surprised he didn't put some clause in his will, forcing me to live there for the rest of my life.

NANCY

Well he didn't, so you're free to move wherever you want.

ANNA

Yes. (*A beat.*) Tell me about Haslemere, Nancy. What's it like?

NANCY

(*considers*) It's a lovely town. Beautiful woods all round, historic buildings, good shops, an excellent museum. Everything one could wish for really.

ANNA

And your house?

NANCY

A honeypot cottage, little country garden. Hollyhocks, delphiniums, the kind of roses one's grandmother used to grow.

ANNA

It sounds idyllic.

NANCY

It is in a way. But it's just . . .

ANNA/NANCY

Not Paris.

NANCY

I've felt so alive here. Oh, I intended to go back eventually. I've even booked a plot in the cemetry. In the Natural Burial section.

ANNA

You're having a green burial?

NANCY

I toyed with cremation, and then I remembered Uncle Stanley. We all carted off to Sutton Bowling Green . . . He wanted his ashes disposed of there. So Aunt Mabel duly scattered them to the winds and they all blew back into her eyes. She ended up in Moorfields. – No, a natural burial is far less hazardous. They bung you in a shroud, topple you in and you become a tree.

ANNA

Oh Nancy!

NANCY	Though actually I'm having second thoughts about the shroud. I have terrible visions of all my ex-pupils helpless with laughter. I think I'll plump for a bamboo coffin.

ANNA   I don't think you need worry about it yet.

NANCY   Or perhaps a wicker one would be better. I'd
            feel less like a panda.

            (*Front door bell rings*.)

ANNA   It can't be Charlot yet.

NANCY   What d'you bet it's Madame Boussiron again.
            Re-checking the inventory.

            (*She goes to open the door. It is* RAQUEL. *She is
            looking radiant*.)

RAQUEL   (*coming in*) Thank heaven. I was afraid I'd miss
            you. I bumped into the pharmacist just now and
            he told me you were leaving today.

ANNA   At any minute.

RAQUEL   (*to* NANCY) And he said your ankle was good
            as new.

NANCY   (*sourly*) Did he?

RAQUEL   Splendid. I needn't feel guilty any more. Sorry I
            haven't been in touch but life has been simply
            hectic.

NANCY   We tried to ring you but some incoherent
            foreigner answered the phone.

RAQUEL   Oh that'd be Mr Watanabe.

NANCY   Who?

RAQUEL   Madame Boussiron's new lap dog. He's taken
            my flat.

NANCY   Ah, the Japanese.

RAQUEL   He arrived brandishing an enormous wok. She
            took to him at once.

ANNA   Where are you living now?

RAQUEL   (*impressively*) At the Ritz.

NANCY   Don't tell me. You've found a new man.

RAQUEL   Not so new actually. You'll die of shock! I've
            gone back to Reggie.

NANCY   (*duly astonished*) You mean . . . Number One?

ANNA   I thought you still found him dull.

RAQUEL   I've discovered hidden depths. In fact – don't
            laugh! We're getting married next week.

NANCY   (*laughs*) I don't believe it.

RAQUEL   Cross my heart. Second time lucky.

ANNA   How did it happen?

RAQUEL   He turned up in Paris again, couple of weeks
            ago, and when he heard I'd been chucked out
            of my flat he moved me into the Ritz. He
            couldn't have been sweeter, promised me *no
            strings*.

ANNA   And next thing you know you're tying the
            knot.

RAQUEL   Annie cracking jokes! Paris has done you
            good.

NANCY   Raquel, are you sure you're not jumping the
            gun?

RAQUEL   Positive. We've no time to waste.

NANCY   But isn't marriage going it a bit? Couldn't you
              just . . . co-habit?

RAQUEL   I never thought I'd hear old Prudypants
              advocate living in sin!

NANCY   Nor did I. But if it doesn't work out –

RAQUEL   It will. This time it's for keeps. Dear old Reggie
              is just what I need. I realise that now. The great
              thing is I don't have to make an effort with him.
              He's known me since I was eighteen. I can let
              my roots grow out without worrying, not
              bother to have my legs waxed all the time, go
              down to breakfast without putting my face on.
              He's the sort of man –

NANCY   You could grow old with?

RAQUEL   Not on your nelly! We've got forty years to
              make up for. Well, must dash. I've got a fitting
              for my wedding dress. I just wanted to say
              "bon voyage" and all that jazz.

ANNA   Congratulations.

RAQUEL   Sorry I can't invite you. We're getting hitched
              in Las Vegas.

ANNA   You will keep in touch, won't you?

NANCY   Yes, let me know how things go.

RAQUEL   Don't worry. I'll send you a Round Robin every
              Christmas.

NANCY   (*heavily*) Thanks.

RAQUEL   Au revoir. It's been such fun meeting up with
              you both again.

(*She kisses them both.*)

ANNA   Good luck.

NANCY   Yes. Goodbye, Raquel.

RAQUEL   *Rachel* from now on. I've taken your advice,
              Nancy. Well, let's face it, I'm a bit past fur
              bikinis.

              (*She goes.*)

NANCY   Well someone's happy anyway.

ANNA   I can't help admiring her. The way she grasps
              at life.

NANCY   (*grunts*) Instead of throwing the towel in like
              me.

ANNA   Nancy – I've been thinking. You could stay on
              in Paris.

NANCY   I've been through all that.

ANNA   You could get another flat.

NANCY   I'd never find anywhere a patch on this.
              Anyway it's all arranged now. My tenants have
              moved out of the cottage, the cleaners have
              been in, the committees are queuing up for my
              services. Haslemere awaits me.

ANNA   I'm not suggesting you give up Haslemere.
              Couldn't you have both?

NANCY   I couldn't possibly afford it.

ANNA   (*a beat*) But *we* could.

NANCY   What?

ANNA   Between us.

(NANCY *looks at her.*)

ANNA   If we pooled our resources. I've been thinking
            about it, but didn't dare mention it before in
            case the house didn't sell. But now . . . Mr
            Vane says they've offered a very good price.
            We could find a larger flat – with a lift – and
            keep your cottage in Haslemere too. Then if we
            feel like popping to and fro – there's always
            Eurostar.

NANCY   It's a lovely thought, Annie, but – It's out of
            the question.

ANNA   Why? (*No reply.*) You wouldn't want to share
            with me?

NANCY   No, no. I can think of no one I'd rather share
            with.

ANNA   What then?

NANCY   I know you. You're just being kind.

ANNA   Piffle.

NANCY   You don't want to lumber yourself with another
            old crock.

ANNA   Oh don't be such a misery. You'll talk yourself
            into that bamboo coffin if you're not careful.

NANCY   Wicker.

ANNA   You're not a crock. You need to regain
            confidence, that's all. Like I did. – You'd be
            doing me a favour, Nancy. After all this time
            I'm not sure I'd be very good at living on my
            own. (NANCY *looks at her.*) Besides I've fallen
            in love with, Paris too. Not the romantic Paris
            we used to dream about. Although it is still
            romantic. But Paris today, warts and all – the
            snooty waiters, the rude shop assistants, the
            red tape –

NANCY   The endless strikes.

ANNA   The maniac drivers.

NANCY   Sarkozy!

ANNA   Madame Boussiron!

(They laugh. Pause.)

ANNA   So what do you say?

NANCY   It sounds like having our gateau and eating it.

ANNA   And why not?

NANCY   Isn't it a bit late to change our plans? We're leaving any minute.

ANNA   No, we go home as arranged. I deal with the sale of the house. You get back on your feet, and make your excuses to the ladies of Haslemere. Say you can't sit on any committees as you're going to be in France most of the time.

(NANCY hoots with delight.)

ANNA   Then we come over here and stay in a hotel while we look for the perfect flat.

NANCY   Perhaps in a house in one of those little courtyards we're always admiring. – I can only see one snag.

ANNA   What's that?

NANCY   References. I doubt Madame Boussiron will give us glowing ones.

(They laugh.)

ANNA   I can't wait to tell Charlot.

NANCY   Yes, he'll be thrilled. Still surrounded by Les
                 Dames Anglaises.

                 (*They start to sing the song.* ANNA *holds out
                 her hand to* NANCY *who gets up without even
                 thinking about her leg as they start to waltz.
                 Then, realising, she dances with even more
                 gusto.* CHARLOT *comes in and joins them as the
                 lights fade.*)